44 DAYS OF BEING
HUMBLE

Daily Devotional

Jekela S. Burgess

Published by Mynd Matters Publishing
715 Peachtree Street NE
Suites 200 & 100
Atlanta, GA 30308
www.myndmatterspublishing.com

6-54-957092-1-978 (pbk)

FIRST EDITION

This Book Belongs to:

_____

Date:

_____

*Gifted by: _____

For what shall it profit a man, if he shall gain the whole world, and lose his own soul?

- Mark 8:36

To my mommy for motivating me.

To my entire family for shaping, molding, and keeping me.

I'm learning.

I'm humbled.

A Quick Word

Hey there, Sis—

I'm glad you decided to heal with **me**.

To learn how to do life when you are the STRONG friend and the often distant *or* alone friend...

The reliable friend, the consistent parent, the...*everything*.

I get it.

Life gets hard. It gets unfair.

It's important to have a loyal source, a healing place.

I am here with you.

Often, when things get overwhelming, we don't know where to turn, who to turn to, who we can TRUST with our hurt, deepest feelings, and secrets, and we assume we should be able to get through it alone.

BE HUMBLE, *Sis.*

Life will teach you that you will ALWAYS need somebody.

Life will HUMBLE you!

However, before you seek a SOME "BODY," let us journey through understanding and embodying our *OWN* **purpose** in our lives.

Embracing That...

- Your purpose is not their purpose.
- Your happiness is not their responsibility.
- Your healing is your responsibility.

This journey will lead you through 30 days of TRIUMPH over the ENEMY and an additional 14 days of gaining best practices for creating discipline. Each day includes a hip-hop song lyric (for the culture), a scripture, and words of reflection. I chose the title *44 Days of Being Humble* because humility is a discipline that this beautiful culture needs for us to **become** the best versions of our adult selves.

Along life's journey, humility assists most with helping to differentiate when to build up walls versus the act of setting proper and healthy boundaries. For our culture, the way we think, feel, adapt, learn/unlearn, and, most importantly, identify our own core emotional behaviors is vital to aid our healing.

When discipline is integrated with self-awareness, we gain heightened compassion giving us the ability to create healthy boundaries. We can also grow through life versus building and creating walls of trauma, including emotional neglect. Instead, we can develop emotional wealth.

We could all use a daily affirmation to reset our personal algorithm every now and then.

It Is OK to HEAL.

Let's Vibe!

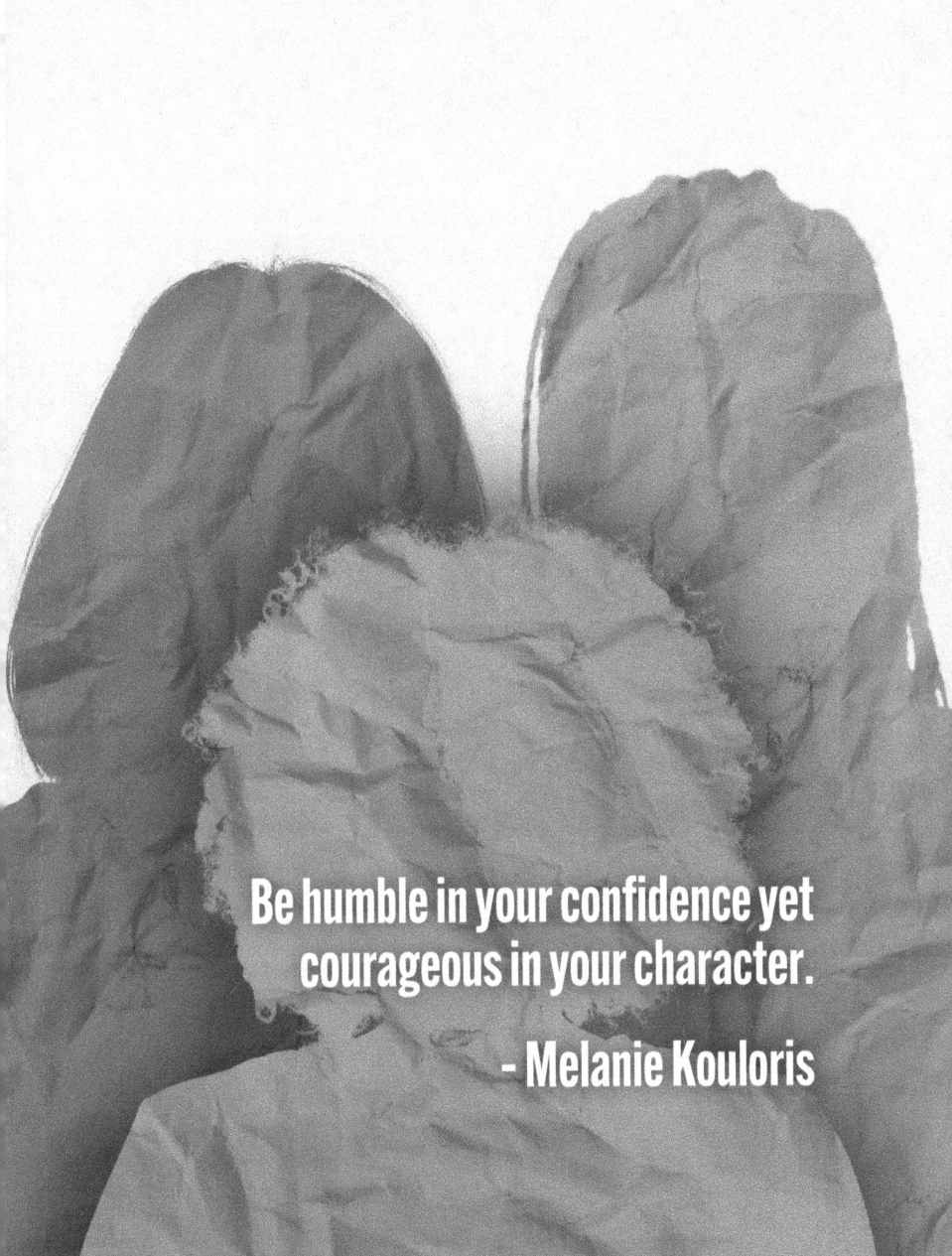

Be humble in your confidence yet courageous in your character.

- Melanie Kouloris

Stay Humble, Stay True

"At 44 mins to 4...
Why aren't you smiling?"
-Jhene Aiko (W.A.Y.S.)

Hebrews 4:16 reminds us, "Let us then come with confidence to the throne of grace, that we may obtain mercy and find grace to help in time of need."

Let us not forget that God will supply all our needs.

So why aren't you smiling?

When we realize God's grace is truly sufficient, we will encounter stages where we get lost in the wilderness. Lord, we pray for the confidence to stand firm and know that YOU ARE GOD, ALONE.

Heal.

The power of healing is one of the most beneficial powers we can embrace. It is the reward for accepting accountability.

The gift of discernment isn't handed to us freely.
Give thanks for every situation.
For God will provide.

Sometimes you must go through the wilderness to reach your true destiny.

> *"There is only one God, and there is only one way that people can reach God. That way is through Christ Jesus, who as a man gave himself to pay for everyone to be free. This is the message that was given to us at just the right time."* (1 Timothy 2:5-6)

It is OK to HEAL

"It's like you got superpowers,
turn my minutes into hours..."
- Ariana G. (P.O.V.)

Time waits for no one, Sis.
Matthew 11:28-30 reminds us, "Come to me all of you who are tired
from the heavy burden you have been forced to carry."

I will give you rest.

"Accept my teaching, learn from me. I am gentle and humble in spirit.
And you will be able to get some rest. Yes, the teaching I ask you to accept
is easy. The load I give you to carry is light."

Move.

It becomes a time when you truly MUST step outside of YOURSELF...
To discover who you are CALLED to be. (Read: Psalm 138:8)

Being who you are "called" to be requires a season of focus. A season
that is going to require your healing to show up as the main priority.
To walk in your purpose, you must understand your assignment. Your
happiness is no one else's responsibility. Don't get lost in your journey.
PAIN WON'T LAST FOREVER.

> *"We have small troubles for a while now, but these troubles are helping us gain an eternal glory. That eternal glory is much greater than our troubles. So, we think about what we cannot see, not what we see. What we see lasts only a short time, and what we cannot see will last forever."*

It Gets Lonely

"Fashion week was more your thing than mine,
I can't even lie… I'd rather stay inside"
- Bryson Tiller (Finesse)

Who doesn't want unconditional love?
Love we know will never leave us.
Not just one that won't leave us,
but one we can trust to never forsake us?

Philippians 4:13, reminds us that Christ is the one who gives us the strength we need to do whatever we must do.

Until your anxiety kicks in and you realize you may not be "ready." The real conversations have happened and now you don't know how to respond. That's Love.

Love Unconditionally

God has created us to have unconditional love and to be loved and accepted, not unloved and rejected. When the people we feel do not love us reciprocally, we inject feelings of unworthiness, instantly thinking we are not enough. This doesn't come easy for most.

God will continuously come up with creative ways to capture our attention. Trying to show us often what we call, signs.

This unconditional, everlasting, perfect love of God is the best love that we could ever encounter.

God's **LOVE is HEALING.**
It is a restoration for our SOULS.

> *"I can do all things because Christ gives me strength."* (Philippians 4:13)

Who do you Love?

"Continue to set the bar,
because they're already underneath it"
- Jason Lyric (Self-Love)

That's the line that stands out in the lyrics spoken by R&B artist, Jason Lyric.
Reminding us how, "God took His time with YOU..."

Love Yourself!

Song of Solomon 4:7 reminds us, "You are altogether beautiful, my love; there is no flaw in you."

What if your self-hate outweighed your self-love?

Chill then Heal...

Not because of the way you have made yourself feel,
Heal in regards of how others left the impression of what love felt like.

Broken promises from broken people.
Your fault or theirs?
It is ok to reflect, just don't stay there.
Loving yourself requires daily practice.

The Equity Theory, in regards to healing, can open your mind to two primary components: *inputs and outcomes.*

Be in a space to receive.

IT GETS UGLY.

> *"So God created mankind in his own image, in the image of God he created them; male and female he created them."* (Gen.1:27)

Ready for War

"They say the truth ain't pretty,
but coming from your pretty mouth"
- Jhene Aiko (What A Life)

What a Life.
He WILL sustain you.
Psalm 55:22 reminds us to, "Give your worries to the Lord, and he will care for you. He will never let those who are good be defeated."

Defeat.

Who *wants* to lose?
How can you ensure to win?

Learn to ALLOW God to fight all your battles.
Not just the ones you find to be "too difficult" for you.
He will take care of you.

"Trusting the process" isn't always a safe place for me.
I was fearful.
I didn't trust a soul.
For what?

When «life» started happening, I didn't understand the point of opening up to everyone around me.

At one point, I was so focused on access only, because...why not?

Pack Light

"How you gonna throw it all away?
How you gonna sit and act like it was nothing... "
- Summer Walker (No Love)

Walking away from something you believe in…

Could you? Would you?

Psalms 16:11 reminds us that you will teach us the right way to live.
Just being with you will bring complete happiness.
Being at your right side will make me happy forever.

Gratitude.

The power of gratitude is beyond measure.
Think of this as your exchange for his continuous mercies.
We give thanks in situations that He has brought us out of. How often do we exchange gratitude for His everlasting grace and mercy?

His mercies are new each day.
Give thanks.

Have you recently taken the time to consider/review your triggers or even your breaking point? Allowing yourself to feel every emotion is hard enough, not reacting to every emotion is even harder. When life started happening, I didn't understand the point of opening up to everyone around me.

> *"He protected us on our entire journey and among all the nations through which we have traveled."* (Joshua 24:17)

Hold On

"...and hold on, hold on...don't let go."
- Teyanna Taylor (Hold On)

Once you realize that the journey you are on is completely yours, you may take a slower approach.

Psalm 18:30 reminds us that God's way is perfect!
The promise of the Lord has proven to be true.
He is a shield to all those who take refuge in Him.

Endurance.

When things get hard, stay consistent.

We freely find the resources to push through for others but limit our own ability to tap into it when it comes to how we treat OURSELVES. Too often, we give up.
We never seem to allow the capacity or opportunity to commit the time, energy, money or efforts that we would offer to a stranger.

Learn your purpose.
Walk in it.

Have the endurance to run your own race. Allow yourself divine permission to heal and train your mind to understand your purpose.

Knowing your purpose is an altitude of Grace.

> *"Blessed is the man that endureth temptation: for when he is tried, he shall receive the crown of life, which the Lord hath promised to them that love him."* (James 1:12)

I'm free

"...I'm Free,
I'm human but I'm comfortable with me"
- Perri Jones (FREE)

How does walking in your purpose look? How does it feel?

John 8:32 reminds us, "You will know the truth, and the truth will make you free."

Lonely.

It's not supposed to feel crowded at the top but at what point do you invite company?

Remember, God will meet you right where you are.

The moment you feel inadequate about getting to the place where you see yourself, remind yourself, "His ways are not my ways." Therefore, you may face detours. Your path may be interrupted. Your destination may not even be the desired location you have sought for yourself this entire journey. Then what?

> *"Just as a body is one whole made up of many different parts, and all the different parts comprise the one body, so it is with the Anointed One."* (1 Cor. 12:12)

I THANK YOU in advance, in moments like these.

I trust to LEAN not on my own understanding after realizing I had no understanding of what HIS will was versus mine.

Hold on, stay free in the spirit of truth.

Stay Humble. Be Humble.

"This is the peace that you cannot buy"
TEMS

…It's ironic that on DAY NINE, I ran across something titled,

9 BIBLE verses that will give you peace of mind:

I immediately wanted to share the list.
1. Isaiah 26:3
2. Philippians 4:7
3. John 16:33
4. Galatians 5:22
5. John 14:27
6. Colossians 3:15
7. Romans 14:17
8. Ephesians 2:14
9. Joshua 1:9

Living by Faith
For this reason we do not lose heart: Even though our outward man is perishing, yet our inward man is being renewed day by day.

I'm not sure how or why this came up but it gave me complete assurance that:

*God is **WITH** me and **FOR** me no matter what!*

Heavy on Alignment

"I don't relate to you (no, I don't)
I don't relate to you, no…"
- ASTN (Happier than Ever)

Who can you relate to, Sis? Stay humble.

Isaiah 40:29 reminds us:
He helps tired people be strong.
He gives power to those without it.

Focus.

This world is designed to bring distraction in the same form that caught our mere attention.

Its ok, it's HOW YOU RESPOND.

Being in a position where you are either comparing or being compared, is the social media influence that we are currently under.

What is the benefit of comparing? How does that really make you feel? In addition, ask yourself, Why does this make me feel this way? Is it the victory?
Is it the recipient?

Gain knowledge and seek discernment within to understand how to respond.

> *"Trust in the Lord with all your heart and lean not on your own understanding."* (Proverbs 3:5)

Check Mate

"I wanna love you in every kind of way"
- H.E.R. (In Every Kind of Way)

We must love ourselves first.

Matthew 6:27 reminds us, "You cannot add any time to your life by worrying about it."

That overthinking is going to kill you, Sis!

Humble.

Trusting God to supply ALL your needs is where it's at!

There is nothing out there that can equate to the physical, mental, emotional or financial SUPPORT and protection that our God can provide.

> *"Therefore do not worry about tomorrow, for tomorrow will worry about itself. Each day has enough trouble of its own."* (Matt 6:34)

Trust the Process

"You gotta bear with me"
- Teyana Taylor (Bear With Me)

Romans 13-8:12 reminds us, "Therefore, brothers and sisters, we have an obligation—but it is not to the flesh, to live according to it."

Endurance.

Bear with me, to what degree?

To what extent can you wait for a person, Sis?
What are your true limitations when it comes to "waiting?"

I've learned there is no benefit in leaning on your own understanding.

Sis, you will never figure it out. Your ways are not His ways. His ways are not your ways.
Bear with me.

Watching reality TV dating shows together became one of our habits. While doing this, it was apparent that insight was truly needed. An outside perspective of what it looked like, retrospectively DATING other people. A benefit was that the activity showed me that my partner was as just as committed as I had been to "getting it right." It was a beautiful thing.

However, it also opened doors and conversations that became completely uncomfortable to approach. How long can we truly wait for others to open up? To meet the other person halfway? To change? Bear with them, huh?

HUMBLE (af)

"baby, baby, baby... I've seen us on the first day"
- Alicia Keys (You Don't Know My Name)

In every romantic relationship that I've encountered. I took a specific approach.

Cor. 12:9, reminds us, "But he said to me, My grace is sufficient for you, for my power is made perfect in weakness." Therefore, I will boast more gladly about my weaknesses, so that Christ's power may rest on me.

I was both proud of this and upset.
Upset recognizing later, that I am very apparent and forthcoming of every and anything that I want.

If I want it, I will get it.

Later, as I grew in the relationship,
I started to wonder if I, too, was what they "wanted" in return?
Was this enough?
Did they settle because life was good?

I still credit myself, completely, in being transparent in knowing and expressing what works for Me.

Catch what I said there Sis...what works for ME.

Mine

"...blessed is the woman, who's got a man like mine..."
- Shirley Brown (Blessed is the Woman)

Psalm 9:10 reminds us, "Those who know your name trust in you, for you, Lord, have never forsaken those who seek you."

Realizing what you have in life versus what you feel you deserve becomes a challenge. The goal is to accept that what you have is everything you need.

Unfolding every benefit reaped in the harvest of God's abundant Garden of Life means reaping all of God's promises to fulfill your harvest.

THE ART OF GRATITUDE IS A MASTERPIECE.

Ready

"I may be young but I'm ready..."
- Beyoncé (Party)

Moving forward, life will often remind you to never lose sight but to focus on yourself.

Proverbs 3:5 reminds us, "Trust in the Lord with all your heart, and lean not on your own understanding."

Wait.

If you don't understand, always remember that it is OK not to know UNTIL you DO know.

This is where most people lose sight. As humans, we desire the need to know. We like to sound informed and competent when we speak. While there is nothing wrong with having confidence, it benefits no one to be loud and wrong. Basically, just hush. Stay humble enough to know you were not designed to know it all. The resources are there.

GAIN KNOWLEDGE AND GIVE THANKS. GRATITUDE IS KEY.

Clones

"See, most you people move like clones.
That's why I be on my own"
- Tobe Nwigwe (I'm Dope)

Making it home meant more to me than you knew or it even sounded.

If my friendships were DISTANT, I would have to learn to commute and adjust. Each time I pray hard and humbly that I just make it back home safely in the return.

Colossians 3:12 reminds us, "Put on therefore as the elect of God, holy and beloved, bowels of mercies, kindness, humbleness of mind, meekness, long-suffering."

Humility.

Be humble.
(Stay true).
Stay humble.
(Stay true).

This is an affirmation I created, realizing that when the devil can't take your Competence, he is still in reach to take your Confidence.

...only if you let him.

Nothing Wasted

"Those innocent eyes..."
- Miguel (Girl with the Tattoos)

When the emotional connection is gone, let go.

God reminded Samuel of the mastery of moving on. Be reminded that once God is done with it, it is still DONE.

"Fill your horn with oil and go down to Jesse's house."
This is NOT the season to waste your oil.

Psalm 56:8 reminds us, "You know I am very upset. You know how much I have cried. Surely you have kept an account of all my tears."

Move Forward.

If you stop crying about your past, God will show you everything on the way for you.

Stay Humble, Stay True

Morally Speaking

"Show my love for you, can I show my love for you"
- Drake (Yebba's Heartbreak)

Moral Attack.

Being able to receive is not the same position you are in when giving. God reminds us that he will use people for His purpose based on His criteria and moral standards.

Thank God in advance for trusting us in our imperfect seasons. John 1:5 reminds us, "The light shines in the darkness, and the darkness hasn't overcome it."

IMPERFECT.

What is perfect?
What does that really mean?

Objectively, the story of Saul and David is here for our learning. Saul lost his "job." David kept his "job." God was showing us that he could use people who are imperfect but would use them solely because he can TRUST them. David made a lot of mistakes, but God trusted him.

Understanding how to operate in a space where you can be your complete self is amazing. In a world where everything seems perfect, be yourself. Everyone else is taken.

"A Masterpiece trying to Master Peace."

Kiss Me More

*"...will you kiss me more, we're so young,
Boy we ain't got nothing to prove..."*
- Doja Cat (Kiss Me More)

Most relationships (of any kind) require work. It's that simple.
There will be good days, bad days, sick days and the best days you
have ever seen.

Psalm 46:1 reminds us, "God is our refuge and strength, a very
present help in trouble."

Present Help.

Don't forget to show gratitude for everything, and I do mean
everything, you already have.
The act of humility teaches us to understand that the same way we
receive a "good thing" may be the same way we lose it.

God is truly good all the time and all the time, God is *truly* GOOD.

GIVE THANKS.

Embrace Peace

"This is the peace that I couldn't buy."
- Tems (Free Minds)

Compromising your peace is one of the most dangerous things that one can do. Understanding the peace that you already have is so important on this journey called life. Not knowing exactly where your energy aligns can alter your way of thinking. You may become stuck in the wilderness.

James 4-1:2 reminds us, "Consider it pure joy, my brothers and sisters, [a] whenever you face trials of many kinds, because you know that the testing of your faith produces perseverance. Let perseverance finish its work so that you may be mature and complete, not lacking anything."

Compromise.

The scripture reminds us that danger is always near. Instead of seeing this as a negative approach, be reminded that the Lord's hand is always in it.

This is a peace that I couldn't buy.

Putting my trust in anyone else knowing that those words have been written, would be a compromise to my soul.
I feel it.

God's grace is so sufficient.

They that Wait

"...and I don't understand BABY, why can't you. WAIT FOR ME."
- Realestk (Wait for Me)

Waiting for anything is contingent on the person.

If I told you I am waiting for you, how would this be perceived? If someone asks you to wait for them (in return), how long would you wait?

2 Peter 1:3-4 reminds us, "His divine power has given us everything we need for a godly life through our knowledge of him who called us by his own glory and goodness. Through these, he has given us his very great and precious promises so that through them you may participate in the divine nature, having escaped the corruption in the world caused by evil desires."

Ego Driven.

In order to properly understand how to receive such a heavy request, first seek discernment. When you are blessed, your greatest challenge will be the opportunities you face. You can't lose.

Being able to discern ego vs soul will allow an unexpected discipline that will *humble you.*

Choose your Soul.

No Love

"I just want to be everything you need. I wish you could see how you ARE HURTING me"
- Summer Walker (No Love)

Sis, no one can determine YOUR happiness. You cannot MAKE people happy.

Joshua 1:5-6 reminds us, "No one will be able to stand against you all the days of your life. As I was with Moses, so I will be with you; I will never leave you nor forsake you. Be strong and courageous because you will lead these people to inherit the land, I swore to their ancestors to give them."

Courage.

The history of the legendary story, *The Wiz*, never made more sense until I understood the main characters. Consider the Cowardly Lion, a character that needed a whole heart.

He was a victim of disorganized thinking.

The problems were never anything other than the fear of failing.

There were three profound lessons for the Lion to complete his journey. Lessons two and three came by way of the actual journey (similar to escaping from the wilderness).

Stay Humble.

I'm (really) Dope

"See most these Sheeple, they move like Clones,
that's why I be on my own."
- Tobe Nwigwe (I'm Dope)

I have never tried to fit in; I don't see that I ever will. I love it here.

Ephesians 4:23 reminds us, "Be renewed in the spirit of your mind."

New Friends.

Realizing your own power will forever help to contribute to any bonds you create. In the words of Fabolous, *"I'm a movement by myself but I'm a force when we're together."*

Those are facts, scientifically speaking.

As a noun, Force can be described as the STRENGTH or energy as an attribute of physical action or movement.

As a verb, it means to make a way through or into by physical STRENGTH; To break open by force.

Being able to assist with moving someone or something closer to what they believe in is powerful.

That's Love.

Humbly Speaking.

Boundaries

"Here's what we not gone do
...when we're in love."
- Andy Mineo (Not Gone Do)

Have you ever had someone stand firm in who they are or believe themself to be?

TRANSPARENCY *should* be REQUIRED in anything we do.

Philippians 2:3-4 reminds us, "Do nothing out of selfish ambition or vain conceit. Rather, in humility, value others above yourselves, not looking to your own interests but each of you to the interests of the others."

Fair Game.

Healthy boundaries allow each person in a relationship or family to communicate their wants and needs, while also respecting the wants and needs of others.

Learning how to separate and empathize with someone else's needs over your own is key.

This will humble you.

Where there are unhealthy boundaries, safety in the relationship is compromised. This may lead to dysfunctional relationships, where people's needs are not being met.

Jungle Life

"... It feels like a jungle when I'm with you.
Rock me real slowly..."
- H.E.R. (Jungle)

The comfort of being wanted and you feeling it, is an astronomical force. *Not to be confused with what looks good vs what feels good vs what is good.*

Ephesians 5:6-7 reminds us, "Let no one deceive you with empty words, for because of these things the wrath of God is coming upon the sons of disobedience. Therefore, do not be partakers with them."

Stand Out.

The scripture was clear. The instructions to stand out are written.

The quickest way to define the jungle is life or death.

Surviving is First.
Next, learning discipline enables us to Strive.
Then, learning how to feed your hunger allows us to Thrive.

Body

"I don't know what it is, I can't tell you what it is; but you got me going crazy, what you do is so amazing"
- Summer Walker (Body)

John 8:7 reminds us, "So when they continued asking him, he lifted himself up, and said unto them, He that is without sin among you, let him first cast a stone at her."

Alignment.

My mind, my body, my heart.
When one element is OFF, they are all off.

You feel it.

In your heart, there is an emptiness.
Your mind wanders more.
Your body will shift.

If love is your SUPERPOWER, you will feel it. There is no way around it. No one should ever tell you to shun your SUPERPOWER.

Shine.

It is a constant reminder that your peace is also being compromised. Allow yourself the proper alignment when one of your energies adjusts.

Harvest

"God bless, I think I'm insane"
- Summer Walker (Insane)

Isaiah 30:18 reminds us, "Yet the Lord longs to be gracious to you; therefore, he will rise to show you compassion. For the Lord is a God of justice. Blessed is all who wait for him!"

Patience.

We have so much integrity when it comes to everyone but ourselves. We even have the agility and patience to wait for another human being.

BUT...
They that wait on the Lord.

I will be forever grateful to have the assurance of knowing that I have a Constant Companion. I will never be alone.

The fear of being alone is something I never predicted as a personal fear until I was there and understood its depth.

...but God.

Harvest

"I would forever ever be grateful."
- Mahalia (Grateful)

Being humble and staying humble are two separate acts of grace.

NEITHER are for the weak.

Psalms 77:1-2 reminds us, "I cry out to God for help. I cry out to you, God; listen to me! My Lord, in my time of trouble I came to you. I reached out for you all night long. My soul refused to be comforted."

Humility.

When we say, "Be Humble," what does that really mean?

I had to learn to separate His grace from His daily mercies. This was also taught in a spiritual form of not leaning "on my own understanding."

Trust God in everything you do.

Humbly,

Trust in the Lord with all your heart, and lean not on your own understanding; in all your ways acknowledge Him, and He will direct your paths.

Solid Ground

"Don't leave, it's my fault, cuz you make my Earfquake..."
- Tyler the Creator (Earfquake)

WHO's to really blame when there is someone to fault?

Psalms 77:11 reminds us, "Lord, I remember what you have done. I remember the amazing things you did long ago."

Blame Game.

Placing blame on a situation is easier than it sounds.

However, being lost in translation or stuck in your feelings will have you forgetting how to praise Him for ALL He has already done.

We are not built to be "yes men" or "yes women." There will be times when we will not always agree.

In this life we will be disappointed.

This does not make one wrong vs. right.

STAY HUMBLE.

Stay true and most importantly, stay consistent.
He has been faithful BEFORE.
He certainly will be faithful AGAIN.

It is What It Is.

"She said what if I'm afraid to fall in love,
cuz what if it's not reciprocated?"
- Pink Sweat (Honesty)

John 3:16 reminds us, "Yes, God loved the world so much that he gave his only Son so that everyone who believes in him would not be lost but have eternal life."

As we grow through life, we will come to terms that life isn't always fair, nor reciprocated.

Therefore, learning the power of forgiveness and how to apply it is ideal for LEARNING reciprocation.

Reciprocation.

1A: *a mutual exchange*. 1B: a return in kind or of like value.
2: an alternating motion.

Ultimately, the expectations of what is looking to be received are clearly based on what is being put out.

There is no other way around it.

Always be intentional in the energy you put out and look to receive.

Remember, my God will use his glorious riches to give you everything you need. He will do this through Christ Jesus.

Ego kills knowledge, as knowledge requires learning, and learning requires humility.

- Rolsey

MIND DETOX
Discernment/Praying/ Fasting

For there is a God who sits high and looks low. Just chill.

Just as there are numerous intervention approaches to enhancing psychological well-being, there are also strategies for enhancing spiritual well-being, including nondenominational guided imagery, music, journal writing, and, most importantly, understanding how to gain/maintain a *continuous* discipline for yourself.

Along with gaining a practice of your own, remembering mind, body, and soul healing. Training the entire body to respond to the way of thinking.

Mental Detoxing is the process of clearing and cleansing the negative, unnecessary, and unconscious thinking that impacts our mental, physical, emotional, and energetic well-being.

Its important to take intentional steps and practices to soothe your soul and make the most of your time.

Ask yourself: *"How is your Sleep"*

Ask yourself: *"Where is your Focus"*

Ask yourself: *"Am I being Mindful"*

Confirm: *When is the last time you took a walk?*

Release / Talk about it

Organize your Space / Clean up

Put on some **music**

Unfocus / Relax…please.

Detox from people

Acknowledge your feelings

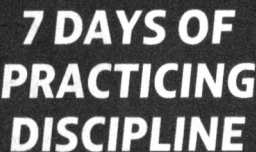

7 DAYS OF PRACTICING DISCIPLINE

Are you truly up for a challenge against your own humility?

Day One:
Recognize your strengths/weaknesses. It's time to check yourself.

Day Two:
Discern what is important to you. Make time for YOU.

Day Three:
Create a plan. Learn your body and pay attention to its signs.

Day Four:
Don't complain…for the day, at least.

Day Five:
Set a goal using a six-month plan.

Day Six:
Set boundaries.

Day Seven:
Write down positive statements for and about yourself.

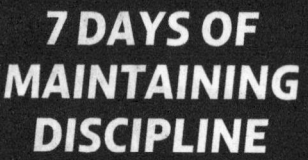

7 DAYS OF MAINTAINING DISCIPLINE

Photo/Selfie Challenge

Day One:
No social media / Go outside.
Take a picture of the prettiest outdoor scenery
for the day.

Day Two:
Find joy in the small things.
Take a picture of something that gives you joy.

Day Three:
No junk food. Take a full-body photo of yourself.
The transformation starts now. Thank me later

Day Four:
Drink water. Drinking water daily is rewarding.
Take a picture of something that gives your peace

Day Five:
Create art. Take a picture of your new artwork or a new
accomplishment.

Day Six:
Speak to someone new today.
Take a picture with them or of them.

Day Seven:
Date yourself. Show us your food through
images. #INDULGE

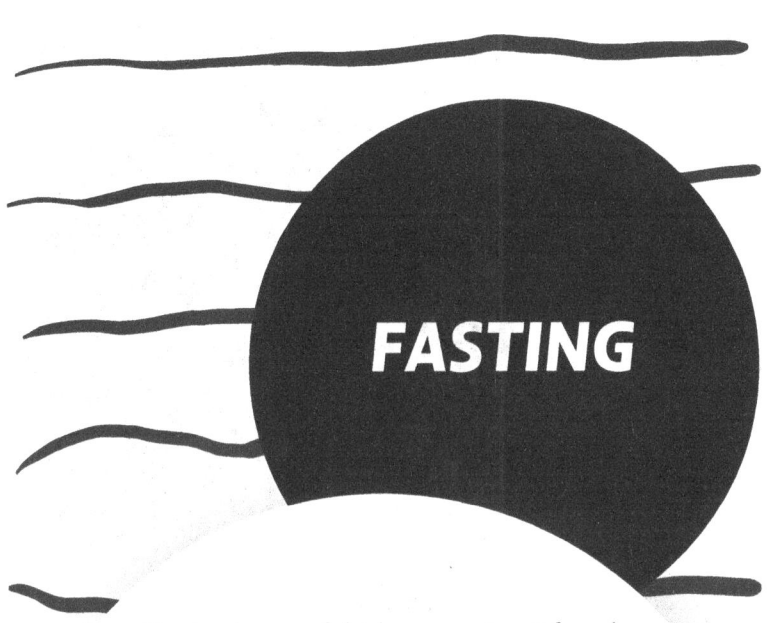

FASTING

Fasting is one of the best practices I found
to provide conscious results. There are several
forms of fasting. However, the practice taught me
how to obtain as well as maintain a daily practice that
was committed and devoted to myself versus a commitment
to others.

Enforce the same **integrity** you have for others with yourself.

Your mind is connected to your body which means you will
have constant reminders of how to recognize when your body
needs to cleanse.

"...the more you heal, the finer you get..."
- Kela

SOUL ADJUSTMENT
(Soul Search)

Our soul›s purpose is,
first, to **remember the truth of who
we are and then share that with the world**.
It is a feeling rather than a physical thing. It is why
we do something rather than what we do. Here are ways
we can allow ourselves soul purpose alignment.

Being in touch with the ego reminded me that in the duration
of my life journey, there was never a lack of *love*. Pure love was
always encompassing me.

In the journey of life, we involve ourselves in situations where a lot of
spaces that we enter are ego-driven spaces versus safe, organic spaces.
The love is there, but not as pure or maybe not even purposeful as
your soul receives.

When the ego separates from the soul. There is peace that truly
passes all other understanding because you are now en route
to an inspired purpose versus a planned destiny.

- Stay Humble

*"His will is not your will. His ways are
not your ways."*

> **Without the ego, there lies inspiration vs. possession.**

1. It is ok to Heal

2. Cry *(you'll make fewer tears as you get older)*

3. Be Intentional / Be Clear

4. Be Present *(in where you are in your journey)*

5. Read more

6. Listen to Podcasts

7. Go Outside
*(spending time in nature has been found
to help with anxiety and depression)*

8. Meditate *(gain mindfulness)*

9. Practice Gratitude

10. Smile

Without humility,
there can be no humanity.

- John Buchan

Humble Thoughts

Stressed is Desserts spelled backward.
Indulge—it's good for you.

Dentists have recommended that a toothbrush be kept
at least 6 feet (2 m) away from a toilet to avoid airborne
particles resulting from the flush.

There are more than 1,700 references to gems and precious
stones in the King James translation of the Bible.

Just so you know: 111,111,111x111,111,111=
1234567897654321

Charlie Brown's father was a barber.

The word «nerd» was first coined by Dr. Seuss in
If I Ran the Zoo.

You burn more calories sleeping than you do watching TV.
Get some rest.

Children grow faster in the springtime.

The elephant is the only animal with four knees.

Goodbye came from "God bye" which came from
"God be with you."

In the words of the LEGENDARY Nipsey Hussle,
"The marathon continues."

Stay humble, stay true...the life you choose is yours.

*Congratulations on believing in yourself
and taking the time to engage and inspire.*

*If you were inspired by this book in any way,
feel free to share.*